Uncharted

June Hall lives in the heritage city of Bath with her novelist husband, Greg. Her son, Richard, lives and teaches in Spain, and her daughter, Katherine, lives and works in London. She began her career in the editorial department at Faber & Faber where she eventually became an editor before moving into paperback and American publishing and eventually setting up a literary agency which 10 years later in 1988 was to merge with the giant agency, Peters Fraser & Dunlop.

Major life events have inevitably shaped the subject matter of her poetry – in particular the stillbirth of her first son, Philip, in 1987, and the diagnosis in 1997 that she had Parkinson's Disease. Both led to writing poetry and publishing it in various magazines. This is her third collection, following *The Now of Snow* in 2004, and *Bowing to Winter* in 2010. She also co-edited *The Book of Love and Loss* with R V Bailey.

All her books so far have contributed a percentage of the sales revenue to current research into Parkinson's Disease and this is no exception except that it will double the past donation from 50p to £1 per copy sold.

Also by June Hall

The Now of Snow

'Every poem is different yet all bear the stamp of her compassionate vision. The forms of her poems are as varied as their subjects.' **U A Fanthorpe**

'The book's title suggests transience, while the poem of that title fixes the importance of a single, shining moment….Each poem, true to the book's epigraph from the teachings of Zen master, Thich Nhat Hanh, embraces a present moment.' **Ann Drysdale**

Her gift for keen observation enables her to capture the moment and bring wry humour and courage to the familiar and the darker places of life. **Maggie Butt**

Bowing to Winter

'Reading this collection is a moving experience, providing remarkable insight into an experience of illness and grief, and certainly *making them new*. These are strong, original poems.' **Emily Wills**

'June Hall writes vividly and well about almost everything that frightens us… This approach helps her write about her own Parkinson's disease… But truth-telling would not be complete if the poet ignored life's delightful moments – and she doesn't.' **Dilys Wood**, *Artemis*

'Her poems are positive and life-enhancing, even when the poem describes, often in harrowing and stark language, unhopeful and complicated futures with a truthful reality. She talks about permanence and change and gets both spot on.' *Focus/Acumen*

'I do like her work – it has tremendous punch and manages to be both humorous and tragic simultaneously.' **Wanda Barford**

The Book of Love and Loss
(ed. R V Bailey and June Hall)

'Dedicated to the memory of U A Fanthorpe (1929-2009), summed up in the introduction as *a pacemaker for the broken heart*, and featuring such poets as Gillian Clark, Jacky Kay, Carol Ann Duffy, Andrew Motion, U A Fanthorpe, Mario Petrucci, Philip Gross, Penelope Shuttle, Ann Drysdale and Roger Elkin, this handsome, almost 400-page anthology promises *a fresh approach to a universal theme* from 197 contemporary poets, and it doesn't fail to deliver that promise.' **Jan Fortune**, *Envoi*

Uncharted

JUNE HALL

BELGRAVE PRESS • 7 BELGRAVE ROAD • BATH • BA1 6LU

Copyright © June Hall 2016

First published 2016 by
Belgrave Press, Bath
7 Belgrave Road,
Bath,
BA1 6LU
UK

NO UNREQUESTED SUBMISSIONS PLEASE.
THANK YOU.

LEGAL NOTICE
All rights reserved. No part of this publication may be reproduced, stored in a retrieval system, or transmitted, in any form or by any means, electronic, mechanical, photocopying, recording or otherwise without the prior permission in writing of the publisher.

Requests to publish work from this book must be sent to Belgrave Press, Bath.

The moral rights of the author are asserted in accordance with the Copyright, Designs and Patent Act, 1988

A catalogue record for this book is available
from the British Library

ISBN 978-0-9546215-3-7

Designed and Typeset by John Hawkins Design 07780 502417
Cover design by Paul Mitchell Design Ltd 01628 664011

Printed in Zrinski d.d., Croatia

Acknowledgements

Thanks to the editors of the following magazines in which one or more of my poems have appeared: *Acumen, Agenda, Artemis, Coffee House Poetry, De Facto, Equinox, Envoi, First Time, French Literary Review, The Interpreter's House, Iota, Orbis, Poetry Nottingham International, Poetry Salzburg Review, Poetry Scotland, Seam, Staple.*

The Lady Who is Not for Turning was highly commended by Second Light in one of their Long Poem Competitions; *Verdict* won 1st place in an Award for *Orbis* Readers; other poems were shortlisted for the Bridport Prize in 2013 and for the Mervyn Peake Award; *Yellow Bird* was voted Poem of the Month at Second Light.

Several poems appeared in *First Sixty* (Acumen Publications, 2010) and poems have appeared in other anthologies: *Get Me Out of Here* (2011); *Cracking On* (2009); *Running Before the Wind* (2013, all ed. Joy Howard, Grey Hen Press); and in *Shades of Meaning* and *Outlook Variable* both ed. Joy Howard, Grey Hen Press, 2014) Five poems – *The Now of Snow, Real Estate Tango, Bath Time, Little Man* and *Mrs Dribbles* – were collected in the CD, *On Being Human* (Poppy).

Huge thanks are due to Rosie Bailey – a kindred spirit and fine poet. She was at all times helpful, encouraging, enthusiastic and inspiring, as well as being willing to share much of the work of bringing these poems to print. It is warming too how supportive my colleagues and fellow poets have been – as have many workshop leaders and other editors, especially Patricia Oxley.

Thanks are also due to Teresa Skinner, Gill Christie, Chris George and Bob Scott for keeping down the chaos around me and to Cleve Vine, now retired, for all his help and cheerful support over the years with the business side of things. Finally thanks also to my family, particularly Richard and Katherine, both perceptive, exacting, proud and caring critics.

For Mum

1921-2015

Contents

I
Mind the Gap	17
Dead and Alive	18
The Surgeon	19
wind	20
heat	20
virginia creeper	20
the old man	20
June	20

II
Ever After	21
Wonky	22
Burning	23
no ending	24
snowman	24
tears	24
at the end	24
heights	24

III
Beach	25
Picnic Moon	26
Crocodile Blood	27
The Open Door	28
Perverse	29
Death by Mother	30
One Plate at a Time	31

Daughter	32
White-Water	33
Windfalling	34
Up There	35
Leaving Home	36
gap year	37
new graduates	37
badminton	37
bike	37

IV

A Family Silence	39
Non-Graduate	40
Cane	41
We Three	42
nightmare	43
life study	43
no rehearsals	43
cabinet	43
inspiration	43

V

81 Victoria Drive	45
Friends	46
Tim	48
Face Test	49
Rumple	50
Octopus Love	51
too rough	52
the massage that didn't work for you	52
binned	52

VI

Mars and Venus	53
Blowing Cool	54
Decree Absolute	55
Wild at Sixty	56
Parting Shots	57
Inside	58
Voyage	59
Within	60
Summit	61
The When of Tears	62
Smoke Buds in Autumn	63
grey boots	64
reflection	64
high five!	64
Sunday in town	64
losing the day	64

VII

Boom and Bust	65
Chinese Landscape	66
Eruptions	67
Circles	68
Meaning	69
A Real Poet	70
The Lady Who is Not for Turning	71
Verdict	75
on Airforce One	76
the president	76
night poem	76
election	76
stepping	76

VIII

Mrs Dribbles and the Chrome Invasion	77
Mrs Muddles and the Muddly Day	78
Mrs Wobbly is Fed Up	79
If I had Pills Enough…	80
Pain at Midnight	81
What if	82
Suppose	83
Don't	84
It	85
bender	86
work	86
hospital bed	86
geriatric	86
night-drop	86

IX

face	87
angled	87
mother	87
no mother	87
The Hat	88
Mum Comes with Me to Therapy	89
The Good Ship Care	90
A Time to Die?	91
Grab-Handle	92
Just Before Dark	93
Uncharted	94

X

Throssel Hole	95
Walking Backwards	96

God is	97
Eagle Wings	98
Seven Deadly Sins	99
Riddle	100
El Alcazar	101
Just Sitting	102
Walking Meditation	103
The Present Moment	104
Arches	105

All our journeys have destinations of which we are unaware.
    Martin Buber

Full fathom five thy father lies;
Of his bones are coral made;
Those are pearls that were his eyes:
Nothing of him that doth fade,
But doth suffer a sea-change
Into something rich and strange.
    Shakespeare – *The Tempest*

Faith is a bird that feels dawn breaking and sings while it is still dark.
    Old Scandinavian saying

I

Mind the Gap

Early Morning
I took the tube to your birth, shivered
through the push and pull of rush-hour crowds,
all the way to the hospital, Piccadilly and Circle line.

Should I leap on to the platform cradling my bulge
or drop into the divide straddling
knowing and not knowing, life and death?

Yesterday's check-up was routine, the wait
lengthening like silence as we searched the doctor's face.
Non-viable foetus. To be cut out next day.

This is my stop. *Mind the gap!*

Noon
You're delivered by Caesarean, placed in a crib,
A red bud hangs from your tiny nose –
your blood or mine? My love comes in

like breast milk, fast and fizzing against the tightness,
the harbour space of empty arms.
I don't hold you,

your skin translucent, petal-fine.
I fear you might break up.
With a blue blanket we tuck in memories

and nurses put yellow roses in your cot, wheel you away
exclaiming on long bones and how tall you were.
Am I a mother or not?

This is my stop. I do *mind the gap.*

Dead and Alive

I am thirst of the desert,
sting of the sand-cloud.

I am mirage lost in night,
grasslands turned to dust.

Mother or not?

I am nothing. Tears of fear.
I am body-box, human coffin.

Inside, my son – a bump
in shifting sands.

The Surgeon

For Marcus

It must have been hard
to watch that flat, unmoving screen
when I was round and full at last,
and brave to trace
the tiny skull-bones caving in.

In your face I saw it all: the sharp line fall.

Everything was tested, checks run –
routine – boring almost.
What more could we have done
not to meet this image
or hear its soundless scream?

In your face I saw it all: the sharp line fall.

A man uneasy with emotion,
and anyway, hard-pressed to fit it in,
you did your best to grant
my tough request: to stay awake
through surgery so I could hold my child.

In your face I saw it all: the sharp line fall.

But I may cry, you warned,
catching something beyond words.
I let it pass – like the hand that made
a sudden birdlike flutter towards me.
Too stunned to take it, still I felt its squeeze.

In your face I saw it all:
                      heart on call.

wind

A set of steel clips
moors my plastic table cloth
against the mistral.

heat

The sun umbrella,
heavy on its stubborn base,
tilts at us and laughs.

virginia creeper

sneaks, tendrils reaching
pink over roof and fence;
won't knock – slides in.

the old man

A twist of olive trunk,
grey, gnarled and always there,
commands the garden,
centring the space
with sharp-edged cacti
and pale violet agapanthus.
The sprinklers aren't on
yet soon they will wet
your feet and forehead.

June

Sun bleaches the lane.
Geraniums, pertly pink,
wake early in tubs

II

Ever After

Though my grandmother made a bath-time saddle of her knee
so I could ride-a-cock-horse to Banbury Cross, squeezed
me as she walked a teddy bear round and round
my tiny palm-garden; though she rocked and hushed me
like a baby swaddled in a year of rough white bath-towel
and with her meaty, camphor-smelling hands tried
to pummel and will warmth into me, yet, being just six
when my mother left, I thought I'd cry forever.

I was a pigeon-toed skimp of a girl, short-sighted
with a water-curtain face. Even the bells of Old Bailey
could not rebuild my world or quieten my peals.
Gran could not answer my one repeated question –
nor, after such a great fall, could all her fond rhymes
or all her big hugs ever put me together again.

Wonky

You always wore your lop-sidedness with ease, Bear,
a warm brown growl in one eye, a sad brown kiss
in the other. I treasured the introvert-extrovert split
of your character and the way you embraced
such a rich mix of tears, laughs and cheers.

Caught by Parkinson's, with a bent of limp, slouch
and crooked mouth, I'm un-centred myself now.
I still miss your stumpy legs, plump tum and fur
sleeked with the smell of dribbled pear drops.
Most of all I envy the ease of your wonky face.

Burning

Eight years old. Candles on the Christmas tree.
One break-away flame climbs my back,
its hoarse sizzle snatching at my angora cardigan.
Fir tree and white fluff. Smell of burning wool.

A big man, he dives, grabs, rolls me in the rug,
beats me with firm fists. Like Mum kneads dough.
Over and over. My hero. But soon the room smells
un-Christmassy. Mum sobs. Goodbyes are in the air.

He asks for my velvet book. I won't think. Won't.
Too young to decipher codes, I love what he writes:
My candle burns at both ends: it will not last the night,
but o my friends and o my foes, it gives a lovely light!

no ending

wrapped in a year
of rough, white bath towel,
tears won't dry

snowman

one charcoal eye winks
and weeps, smile turns to mush,
your whiteness lost.

tears

a girl starts crying,
surfing all her emotions
to find a way through.

at the end

on the vet's white slab
stroked flop-ears fold. Shot, you sink,
an unset jelly.

heights

clever girls map-read,
check trig points,
head for the summit

III

Beach

Tide has stretched the sand
wide and open as heaven's floor,
soft with sudden light.

*

Stick taps narrow steps
down to the wild waters' opening.
Cream teas behind us.

*

Pool molluscs, marooned
by tide's swift retreat, grip,
beauty tight within.

*

Wet sand-shine mirrors
sweeps of patterned sky above,
shy sun nudging grey.

*

Climbing hand in hand,
nappied toddlers lunge at life.
Careful parents wait.

Picnic Moon

In spring children are in bed
when it sweeps through sleeping daffodils.

Now, loose in a bath of autumn light
the clear moon floats, flaunting its belly.

Bright globes multiply on every lake –
peeping children sneak the fun of night.

Note: In Japan night picnics are held in the autumn to see the moon at its best – see Ryokan's The Autumn Moon.

Crocodile Blood

The Queensland croc is an awesome beast,
that's survived from Triassic times at least
when famous dinosaurs deceased –
though crocodile parents have cannibal ways,
as killing their young for fun displays.

They bask in a tangle of mangrove glades,
their racks of teeth saw the air like blades
clearing the way for reptilian raids,
then float like cargo down the Nile,
luring their kids with a careless smile.

Mum lurks but Dad's for instant slaughter.
He munches on newborn son or daughter,
throws a death-roll - drowns them in water.
The clamp of his jaws deals a killer blow,
five-tonnes pressure when the bite's just so.

Life on the Daintree can be all too brief
when blood floats round in a silent wreath,
and stains the river red with grief.
The Queensland croc is an awesome beast,
that's survived from Triassic times – at least.

The Open Door

One knee weeps blood. His mother hasn't mended it.
Snuffling in a corner through snot-greased fingers,
he watches her drift and blur on waves of smoke
rafting on their giant gym-ball, a blue-moon yogi.

Outside wide-washed dark waits, hides the stars
as midnight and its chimes hover. Inside,
conscious of the storm, he notes the curtains shimmy,
her face empty when Sunday slips into Monday.

Uncurling, he dumps his last small lump of hope,
limps to their stone-square yard, jaw angled,
though he doesn't know it, in his father's way.
Copycat oaths pour round blocked tears.

Bubble-poised, out of time, her smile dies,
blind eyes never blink, breathing doesn't change.
She hardly hears his pain, sworn to the night and
delivered gift-wrapped through the open door.

Perverse

With thanks to Philip Larkin

They'll fuck you up, your blue-eyed kids,
you may not think so but they will.
With their first cry you're for the skids,
they grab your life and leave the bill.

Your mum and dad you fucked up too –
the daily slog cost them their smile.
You howled and puked and made them stew
through years of fights and sibling bile.

Though kids could drown you in despair
yet keep it up, that long, slow crawl.
They'll fume and glare, soft-soap and swear
then call you when their babies bawl.

Death by Mother

Though she kills them with love,
loss of love, grey despair
(having passed on the genes
they can never repair);

and loads them with guilt
as she swipes at their fun
or snarls at their slobbing
when nothing gets done,

then erupts at the fights,
spewing lava-like rage
(she swears just like them
at the *I-don't-care* stage);

though she growls when they shrug
at her slaved-over meals
and barks about health
while lunch cools and congeals;

hot words scorch them all
when she's dog-tired at night
burn them like sulphur
(she knows it's not right)

yet though they're still children,
when they clash knife to knife,
she marvels that somehow
they escape with their life.

One Plate at a Time

Pertuis, 1997

All day the square burns
under Van Gogh's yellow sun
till cobbled twilight

gathers a fine flock
of scattered, white-clothed tables,
corralled for dinner.

We order... and we wait.
Stuffed with bread and giggles,
kids' fancies run wild –

*Did the Chef get drunk
and cut off his working ear?
Is it still bleeding?*

Is he still breathing?
Vite!, they chant, but each course comes
slow as *escargots*,

one plate at a time.
Drunk on a round of hiccups,
they soon fall asleep,

their *entrée* to France
whirled through the velvet-blue night.
Voilà! New joke born.

Daughter

She strolls through her teens, never missing a step,
girl to woman in several bouncy sweeps, the bunnies
on her bedroom frieze transformed overnight
into pop stars, while the hamster's death
makes timely space for clubs, fashion and shopping.

She used to be *petite*, at home in tomboy body.
Now she's grown solid and shapely, her new jacket
tight-fitting, fashionable, though she still snips off
the linen rose, dismissed as Barbie-doll girly.

Inside I feel redundant, old. Outside
I skip with pride.

White-Water

Testing the length and breadth of her fears, he skims
down-river at the speed of fury, out-paced by demons;
cocksure, he navigates the high-low head-bursts
of twilight rapids; thinks he can steer round
over-dose, flash-back, memory-loss – and even the drift
of a personality-blank where white-water vitality should be.

At times she stays with him, stroke-for-stroke; at others,
back-to-back, they lean into argument more obliquely.

From one *morning-after* to the next, her mind
twists and somersaults to escape, knowing
he might be tangled in trouble, dragged and drowned
as he tests the length and breadth of her love.

Windfalling

When the orchard is scrunch-deep in windfalls
farmers grapple with the puzzle
of this, their dappled young Cox, an in-between
still on the branch. They worry themselves

their apple, smooth, round, nearly full-grown,
will be selected and boxed with the best –
not caught spinning in a twilight tumble

between safe coddling and a bumpy landing,
bruises, blister spots and scabs already
foreshadowed on that russet-green skin,
because when harvest winds are high

apples shake and drop like hopes of the heart,
orchards turn into theatres of intoxication,
releasing heady smells of juice
as wasps fizz far into broken fruit-flesh.

The smell of disaster is strong
but even windfalls reflect the reddening sun.

Up There

Love is the pain of parting, the warmth
of a damp squeeze. Even with helmet he's
not distanced by height as he bends to me

like a glowing strawberry roan nuzzling
her new foal. Goodbye comes out as
the heave of a heart being tested. Tears roll.

I dry my face for my sugar-loving little fellow,
grown tall on whys and wherefores, who
snuffles over me, all six-foot-three of him.

Leaving Home

Today you're throwing childhood away, slowing only
to chuck it into black, headless sacks, necks drawn tight
with twine, before you, who loped unblinking through

puberty, zoom off to dump your bagged-up past with
its nostalgia of furry trophies, (once so fiercely loved),
freeing you to pack more grown-up things into stacking

crates, strangely infant in primary reds, yellows, blues. I
lumber off (shrunk into gin, wrinkles, an ill-curving spine)
to retrieve and hide mementos from that elfin tomboy stage,

wondering if I too will be put aside some day, while you
leave scores of kisses, orders and a heap of memories.
Metallic, your brave little car roars and leaps into the dark.

gap year

(at 15)

but, darling, if you drop out now
the rest of life may be a gap.
It's late – so please don't let us row
but, darling, if you drop out now
you'll lose the race and then kowtow
to rat-faced men who think you're crap –
my darling, if you drop out now
the rest of life may be a gap

new graduates

leggy, high-heeled girls,
gowned in silk, red and white, sport
cheeky mortar boards.

badminton

net divides the lawn,
tempts competition; leans back
smiling guy to guy.

bike

skin-washed with warm wind,
face brushed with the flow of hair,
you crest the hill. Spin.

IV

A Family Silence

Let's go Dutch, he says, smile laddish, vanity creamed
and combed into hair still dark at eighty.
He stops his old banger at a coffee-shop as though
he weren't my father, hadn't just met me
off a ten-thousand mile flight it had taken me
nearly fifty years to catch. Choking, I say nothing.
Am I on the wrong song-sheet?

I couldn't talk – or walk – all those years ago
when he tossed us out as casually as breadcrumbs,
but giving birth myself has wakened
the family loop that holds us together,
father, daughter, grandchildren. Here we are,

and later he decides, as host, to charm me
with unforeseen twinkles and a roll of jokes
set to warm my unease, break down my guard.
I can't be bought so cheaply over dinner,
or allow him to sweep my anger away
as though he had nothing to explain.
Silence curls round us again;

until my last day. *Let's find somewhere for coffee*,
he whispers, conspiratorial as he clamps
my arm in his. Detached at last, we muddle
into courage and conversation in the café.
A spark of connection ignites, not so much
in our words as in the attempt we make to speak.

Parting: a quick press of flesh, arms, cheeks.
Let's stay in touch, he says, meaning it. *Yes*, I say,
knowing we'll never try this hard again.

Non-Graduate

To fail your BA Fathering is sad –
a senior fresher, you're trying to fit in –
but how to put it? Do I call you *Dad*?

I wasn't two when you left, you cad,
you really think I'd call you *Flynn*?
To fail your BA Fathering is sad.

Daddy's for toddlers; *Flynn* makes me mad -
neither flows off the tongue. Do I bargain
on how to put it or do I call you *Dad*?

Father sounds stiff, a tiny bit trad
with brolly rolled, bow-tie, a taste for gin.
To fail your BA Fathering is sad

but passing takes hard work. I'm glad
it's tough – with nappies, sleep loss, life in a spin.
So how to put it? Do I call you *Dad*?

Those Irish eyes protest you're not so bad.
They're charming cheats but promises wear thin.
To fail your BA Fathering is sad.
How to put it? I'll never call you *Dad*.

Cane

For my estranged father in Australia on his 90th birthday

I sent it to you on a wing and a prayer,
a Fred Astaire-style shiny black cane,
its knob and tip embossed in sterling silver.

Why, even before I shipped it, did I use
the description, *elegant*, awakening fantasies
of bright lights and *an independent air*?

We met only once. This gift was a mistake.
It rapped loudly at the ever-open door of
your vanity – an old rhythm of clicks and twirls,

whirls and taps, of women and affairs, the secret
and the debonair. Although the urge grows
stronger to squash your charms, name the harm

you've caused, your fanfare of effects is strangely
seductive, even at my age. But something, somehow
has changed the shape of things between us.

Today a new routine is playing: you
are hiding in your bed, cane forgotten in the cupboard.
No props can help you now.

We Three

She curled a smile at him, broad as the brim
    of her new-issue hat, the Wrens' tricorn;
He, elegant in tropical white and crisp with charm,
    first made eyes at her, then proposed;
I was the outer-space embryo
    that stunned them both when sperm and egg collided.

My mother, now married, tried
    bottles of gin, hot mustard baths, steep steps;
my father tried teaching and when
    his wife grew round and misery dried up her milk
seduced the art mistress;
    I was the half-starved infant who howled long
and loud enough to tip us all beyond the pull of gravity.

nightmare

Anxiety explodes in gas-green flashes.
He wants me to wake
but I'm crawling deeper into the storm.

Decisions fence me in like acid clouds,
strip my skin, falling
in great white flakes from chest and cheeks.

I lift open lips to the lightning.
Now there is only the wait.
I know what will get me in the dark.

life study

A packet of snaps
trims my life into oblongs,
kind angles, less kind.

Wind in a film. Try again.
Can I live with no thumb smears?

no rehearsals

Why mortgage your life?
No policy stops the shuffling
or a deal of suffering.

cabinet

House of cards, sways, wild,
flattens in a changing wind.
New pack. Crisp. Cut. Deal.

inspiration

Space yourself. Brush your lips,
follow the lines that lead you.
Roll through mists of colour
to let whatever will be be.

V

81 Victoria Drive

For Judith

Your buttercup kitchen, its brightness
cluttered with toys from the attic, is where
you used to start the day: brewed coffee, got cross,
quelled the grandchildren and their minor mutinies;
where you argued the toss, read the paper, giggled
and, always ready to help, planned strategies.
But this kitchen's empty. Nothing starts here now
except the day.

The sitting-room, smelling of mahogany-polish
and open fires, waits for a date to entertain.
The curtains must have been swished shut.
Is that you lingering at the piano,
fingers tiptoeing across the keyboard?
Is that your rusty voice, soaring then falling
into rhythms of ragtime laughter? In the half-light
shadows reach across

    into the hall, where, with its warm wrap
of overcoats, open visitors' book and spare keys,
you always gave us your best hello-hug;
Now it's chilly all chair-lift, burglar alarm
and drifts of undirected letters on the stairs
while the grandfather clock waits to be wound.
That's not you at the front door, is it, letting rip
about the dust. The dust

Friends

20.   I'm a student living in the flat above you.
             You say I'm a night-noise.
     You're a teacher, fussy, owl-sharp, interesting.
           We get to know one another.

22.   Refuge and mentor, you fetch me
             off a late train from Paddington,
     wrap me in your sheepskin coat,
            tell me I'm a chump and feed me chops.

Weeks later. You urge me to buck up,
         fix my broken love life.
   I see I'm buying my mother's belief in fairy tales
         and take your advice.

23.   You wear a long skirt and come
           to my do-it-yourself wedding;
   I'm stronger because you give me the family support
        I long for from my family.

20s. London life is a struggle.
           Paperbacks: not ethical, you feel.
   We row about trash reading, success, the Queen;
         then remember we care for each other.

30.   I'm a literary agent now.
           You begin writing a book –
   apparently it's my fault for encouraging you.
          (That one will run and run….)

Late 30s. You're a catalyst so others live better
         and run a non-violent Gandhi week,
   prodding me into taking risks
         and (shock horror) having babies.

39. My first, Pip, dies. You bring a candle.
         For the birth of the others,
    you're there, masked, travel-weary
         but willing to bond. I feel loved.

40s. I move nearer to Bristol.
         I'm deep into motherhood and frustration.
     You're deep into writing and frustration.
         We miss the connection.

50s. I explore poetry, writing, Parkinson's.
         You encourage me but not
     yourself or your own talent.
         I find this tongue-bitingly annoying.

60. Life is good. We raise a glass to it
         though you will call me young,
    which I hate. We celebrate
         and holiday together.

66. You in your eighties are getting married.
         I go to Italy to be your witness
    and wonder if you're doing it to give my poem
         a happy ending,
                        friend?

Tim

You shine in the rich patina of your mahogany table, gleam
down the long sweep of boards you had crafted;

you slurp and burp over a glass of red in one hand, or is it
Spanish *Fino* for the start or *Marsala* for the end?

Reeling, you catch your heel in one of the bright blue
or red Tibetan saddle rugs you insisted on shipping home;

your grin infects the two Buddha heads on corner plinths,
spreads along shelves to smaller effigies of Hindu deities.

In its absence I feel the strength of your hold as you look
into my being and make me special with your bear hug.

On your breath are the smells of Swaffham Market:
pints of prawns, piles of samphire, draughts of bitter

or in the rubber of green wellies, the tweed of a checked cap,
the Norfolk damp of your Burberry puffer jacket.

At my back I hear you padding across the boards.
Now it is quieter. Your shoes no longer join the line.

That warm embrace is already loosening, though not
your unshakeable enthusiasm. You thought everyone,

everything you befriended, every teacher or guest
was the best. It is you who was the very best of friends.

Face Test

You were simple to read once – God's golden boy,
a dimpled chorister, softly blond, intelligence
burning in sky-blue eyes that ignite devotion.

You learned to play with fire at choir practice
and boarding school, shed your young skin, slithered
with cold-blooded ease through multiple expulsions.

Complex now, you pour yourself into Peter Pan smiles,
your blunt features shadowed by designer stubble,
lips too ripe for trust, grin too knowing for truth.

Adopted is the cold stone of excuse you slide under.
Your blank snake-eyes and forked tongue
are toxic as a cobra's, poised to strike.

Who will guess the well-groomed ending to this tale?
Who will spoil the waiting game when skin,
heraldic, gold, coils into something dark and old?

A sonnet for

Rumple

Replete from jellied packet supper,
belly trusting, soft side upper,
a greeting head weighs down my hand,
it pulls and shifts like pouring sand.
With rhythmic purr, eyes full of fun,
his ermine bib glows, white with sun.
He wears his black with Persian pride
spreading his warmth right down my side

but then the hunter-killer wakes
ruffled from dreams by higher stakes.
He leaps and pounces, leaves me reeling,
chases light pricks round the ceiling;
nods off again, forgets the fight,
fluff-full of majesty and might.

Octopus Love

Some friends are bedrock people, gritty,
hard-edged granite – he scrapes himself
on their truth – but she, soft-bodied, coils
and shapes herself to him so no shell comes

between. Her thin arms, hidden in silky black,
wrap about his shoulders, a fond embrace
for celebrations or she hugs him special
to herself as, caught by the turning tide,

and sliding into darker waters, they spin together,
spiralling too fast, too close, an old fear
that wobbles her lurking in those wide, raw eyes.
One arm waves him gracefully away, another

tightens as on prey, releasing clouds of ink
as she pulls him to the beak mouth
that would finish him were he not able to break out,
begin at last to say goodbye.

Some friends are bedrock people, supports, firm-set.
At times they help him learn to dance alone.
Yet still he loves her soft embrace.

too rough

you startle
from my puppy leap,
afraid I'll break you.

the massage that didn't work for you

Soothing hand too heavy
on your soft-shelled, cratered skull.
Sorry. Meant well, luv.

binned

you unclip friendship,
change me like a hoover bag,
call it letting go.

VI

Mars and Venus

Things have been going wrong lately.
Her shirt damp with un-tended tears,
she clutches and misses his firm hand
as he turns from the cling of togetherness.
Yet now she's in his sights, he mans up
to defend her. Assault-by-questioning

smarts, batters like pellets from an air rifle.
Action Man, he's pleased to score hits
for logic, marking and checking targets
as if to map out and blame the results,
unconscious of the sting and shame she feels.
All she wants is for her Martian to kiss her,

notice how, lost in a mist, her eyes are lakes
that brim but will not drain. She longs only
for him to speak her language, hold
his Venus, read her fears, not like
a man might, by technical interrogation,
but by intuition, like any girl worth her salt.

Blowing Cool

She slips into distance
as the sea from the high coastal path
flattens far off into stillness
glazed by the sun.

In the tiny bubble of time
that shapes his silence,
she cools, smooths and shrugs.
Their giggly summer levels away.

Decree Absolute

A rainbow dips one foot
into their broken lives,
pulls back, shiver-shy,
seeping into the mist
as fear creeps deep
into his shoulder-scrunch
and many-coloured rains
bleed into the land.

Can't mend their marriage
or the tracks they've trampled,
yet pity trickles through her.
Briefly she hunkers down
with him where he's slumped
under the fading bow,
lumpish with resentment,

until at last she slips
away, unhooked,
this water-colour morning,
a fresh-rain mermaid,
before she strips to bathe
in the arc's frail radiance,
wash in the secret scent
of freedom.

Wild at Sixty

Birthday Sonnet

Dance fever glues her to weekly TV,
pins her to *Strictly*, a firm *devotee*.
This do at The Bell is a dream under way,
she, tight in her ballgown, he sleek in DJ.
His bow-tie is floppy in flagrant red velvet,
and dress shirt as ruffled as ruffled can get.
Squeezed at her peril in cut-away dress,
flesh thrills at its glittering silky caress.

How delicious to be the birthday girl, led,
dizzy with spinning – yes – right up to bed.
Alive with the buzz of presents and party,
the night's so high-charge, she plays a bit tarty.
Spirit is willing; flesh slightly slower –
he still hits the spot. Wow, what a goer!

Parting Shots

He left me today – he said it's for good –
took the laptop, the Volvo, a car-full of kids.
Dog bagged his chair. I drank dry sherry.
Quite snug by the fire – if a little bit hairy.

Where Black Cat moults (not where he ought),
I've thrown out my vows for better or worse.
I know what I need now (not what I thought):
a big merry bed and a speedy divorce.

Inside

On the balcony, white with sun, wind ruffles
the red-hot, poppy-printed curtains that screen us.
Coffee is perking inside. An over-large pan
on the holiday stove cradles two eggs, their box torn
to make cardboard egg-cups in the English style.

We say nothing of yesterday's dispute.
I cut soldiers, dip and play with my yolk.
Ears blocked by summer swimming, he's happy
not to face jagged bits or uncooked whites.

Trailing wall-plants drip with tiredness.
Gulls screech and call, surprising us close-to
so large, so full of shit – much of it
falling on our patch of terrace. Indoors –
there is no calm. Toast burns. Juice spills.
We dodge our way through breakfast.

Across a bay fringed with beach and sky,
sea slices into land. The fronds of a yellowing
part-dead date-palm bow low and two small boats
punctuate a bright strip of water beyond
the harbour's refuge, pausing, like commas,
to discover where their passage will take them.

Voyage

In Greek myth there was often a journey to make,
a voyage round the emerald brightness of
island-studded seas where heroes were
delayed by flags, landings, prison.

For us too there was a journey, though
the boat was small and the wind low
as we nosed round the Aegean islands.
All seemed to be over between us –
as Penelope must have thought of her marriage
to Odysseus before the sea-road brought him

back to Ithaca. Near-death, chronic disease,
the grit and grime of unclean argument were
obstacles strewn in our path too. The ending was
never going to be easy – as like Penelope
and Odysseus dodging evening shadows,

we grew more wrinkled and less familiar
to each other. Our stout ship, helm
loyal and dogged, didn't altogether break
as wreckage. Time lingered while we, set

on our more intimate work, improvised
and struggled, navigating past
bare-faced peaks and steeply sloping islands
until new sails once more unfurled
a winter-flowering love.

Within

I don't see it coming,
cruelty,
the tongue-attack
on thin-skinned nerves.

I wake in wreckage
chilled at what's broken,
smell your fear
like fumes in the wind.

Hurt subsides,
something soft is born,
flares small within,
surprising as a flambé

that seals tenderness
unimagined.

Summit

For me it's a long wait, lips
pressed close to the bony cave
of your life-hardened head.

Mule-breath climbs,
labours, panting, until at last
you crest a summit.

Now, maybe, you're going on
to discover the quiet cold
and emptiness

where snow-steps trail and stop.
I am still waiting
but you, of course, are not.

The When of Tears

No tears by request. Don't make a display.
The unspoken code is clear, I now learn
and dream of your coffin sliding away.

You've shrunk to a nothing, skin turning grey,
and sunk beyond pain while waiting to burn.
No tears by request. Don't make a display.

The bad jokes you love die with you today.
I'd laugh at them too if you'd only return
but I think that your coffin is sliding away.

Long shadows whisper of final decay –
you'll leave me two kids, a house and an urn.
No tears by request. Don't make a display.

Your dying stirs grief it's hard to convey.
I mean to plant roses, a signal to mourn
now I'm dreaming your coffin is sliding away.

Wait – cancel that! *He will live*, doctors say.
I can't stop the shakes at this sudden u-turn.
Though no coffin slides, and I'm still on display,
tears stream, unrequested. You wipe them away.

Smoke Buds in Autumn

The garden is ahead of the house
as though it has already decided the question that burns
like our bonfire in the sharp November air.

Summer's snapshots replay inside the house where
beach-balls, bats, windbreaks, tennis racquets litter
the hall, waiting to be thrown out or put away.
Smelling of smoke and worry, we poke at
embers hot on downsizing, and choke on ending
the rich narrative of our Victorian villa.

High sash windows frame a russet revolution
where nature's cycle continues, unflappable,
lit by a palette of trampled colour edging the lawn,
bronze or copper coins that roll and race the wind,
and the streaked tumble and smash of windfalls.

Golden rod, which saluted August
with high-pointed jauntiness, is now bowed low
and mouldering. The ancient grey twist of lavender stalk
has partly broken beneath the weight of unpicked flowers,
and the ground-covering of leafy pink geranium
is pink in memory only.

Spring has tip-toed in on the slide of seasons, precociously
pushing up earth not even composted or bedded in.
Its buds, points and pert green shoots, punctuate discussions,
directing us beyond summer's tubs of limp begonias
or even the crunch and shovel of leaf music lost in flames.

A window opens on the garden. The house leans out, straining
to catch any new points of promise.

grey boots

I smooth their softness.
Silver-buckled, they stand tall
as I once stood myself.
Are they my slash of scarlet
flagged by passing pensioners?

reflection

Every day someone I hardly know frowns
more deeply at me, a stranger
in my mother's mirror. The real me,
un-frowning, recedes and shrinks
down a passage never taken to which
I am constantly saying goodbye
while I feed myself pills and painkillers
and try not to freeze, dribble or mumble.

high five!

Palms swing and clash
like cymbals.
The sound of connection
reverberates
like Sunday silence.

Sunday in town

Speeding round the emptiness of Sunday,
I hear the singing heart of the church spill out,
open-lunged into the summer square.

losing the day

I enact my own drama,
do it my way;
reliving yesterday,
it flies away.

Be still and be present –
there's only one showing
and that is today.

VII

Boom and Bust

(with apologies to Alfred Lord T)

As Wall Street cracks from side to side
the City too's in downward slide;
for all the traders who've half-cried
their massive costs can't be denied,
    and ears are hotly burning.
Some banks are bust, the Footsie's low;
home repossessions start to flow;
accounts are frozen, not by snow,
    though stomachs they are churning.

Down columns on the balance sheet
long rows of big-bang zeros meet.
Till now the profit's been all sweet
for limo'ed fat-cats who will cheat,
    their tax in off-shore earning.
They hedge their funds, routinely lie,
bank pay-offs or a gold goodbye.
On borrowed wealth they live and die –
    our gamblers are not learning.

With snouts in troughs and cash-rich highs,
they merge or level (both nice tries),
but bonuses for sure won't rise,
now *bust must follow boom* applies –
    though they are not for turning.
The crunch (read *crash*) hits hard this land,
its debt so huge, who'll understand
the pound is sinking like the rand?
    Soon bankers we'll be spurning
    and cutting off their earning.

    Austerity's returning.

Chinese Landscape

The brush dances, the ink sings
while the painter weeps and the writer hides
autumnal tears. But some creative impulse
is running away with them.

The brush knows if it just keeps sweeping,
dancing on points, dipping in colour,
then all will be well; and the ink knows
that to race with the paint is not really a race.

They pause together,
so painter is happy, scribe inspired:
the picture of spring will be a visual haiku,
a landscape of discreet perfection.

Eruptions

After Joseph Wright's
VESUVIUS IN ERUPTION
when on exhibition in Bath

It won't do.
There's something ugly,
and quite unlikely,
about all that hell-hot lava pouring
through the picture, a tsunami
of molten rock under a coy moon
forming monster-shapes that threaten
the insubstantial people. Reading
convinces him erupting volcanoes are
like that. He paints them over and over,
seeking reality in imagination.

With peripheral vision we glimpse
the portrait-children who start
to whiz around the gallery
and jump into another life. All around
young scamps leap from gold-gilt frames,
climb out of frills and flounces,
swing under formal canvasses,
sick of patience and posing.

A toddler clenches and buries
a tiny fist under folds of his dress-shirt
and two rumpled bodies cram
together by candle-light, hiding
their squash of bare skin.
Passers-by catch their giggles and winks
and the warm smells of childhood.
Reality and truth are lit up
by a soft eruption
of tenderness

Circles
inspired by a Bridget Riley exhibition at the Tate

                                A wall of circles fills the hall.
                                         They turn,
                                            spin, wink,
                                              geometric
                                                arcs and curves
                                                  that overlap –
                                                   drawn precisely
                                                    to the artist's
                    orders
                        by apprentices
                           who, like
                            boys at work on
                             the Sistine Chapel,
                              fill in detail,

        space and matter,
         shape and void;
        clash and dance together
       in the morning light,
      black on white,
       arching hoops on flat planes.
        They swirl and dazzle
            like sparklers in the night
                 defining the shape
                     of freedom   while the artist sits below,
                                                 down-sized, doll-sized,
                                                   resting, paint and
                                                      masking-tape in hand.
                                                        Plaster cakes her apron.
                                                         She smiles the battered
                                                           smile of one who's
                                                            suffered many art-storms
                                                        in patterns created and lost.
                    Tightly anchored,
                         the circles still bend
                            as if by tidal distortion
                                to find, filter
                                 and let flow
                                 a pathway
                                  to the moon.

68

Meaning

is surely not in the arid desert of literary criticism
or the symmetry of lines that carry sense like freight,
running on parallel rails to a destination scored in black ink.

It's in the trickle of allusion, the ripples of reference;
in the spirit presence of the ancestors, their voices at our back,
their influence echoing in deep roots of words or living shoots.

Meaning breaks out in the hum and song of sound –
the cacophony of consonants clashing,
the euphony of vowels cooing and liquid letters flowing.

It's in the rhythm, rhymes, juxtapositions –
the careful pacing of every word or clump of words
(a science and an art) – when nothing is idle or unnecessary

and even white spaces are billboards of significance.
Meaning cannot be confined – we miss and find and miss it
again and again like a sea-bird riding the wind, visible and invisible,

wings flashing as it rolls. It is, eons old and utterly *now;*
it is in the glory of the ant – and the ordinariness of God.

A Real Poet

I'm not a *real* poet, an Ascot thoroughbred
who trots into pentameters, canters into stanzas
and makes rhymes gallop, whipped on
by well-groomed rhythms;

I'm not a lyrical, romantic poet
whose every page is afloat with imagery
cascading and tumbling in free-flow forms,
sculpture in sound;

nor a luminous poet of the mystical,
probing deep into the living lake of myself
to glimpse far-reaching reflections
in rings of fire.

I don't hold the Classics or the Bible in my head;
I'm not a *real* poet, I'm not a man –
and I'm certainly not dead.

The Lady Who is Not for Turning

On either side the river lie
the roofs of London rising high
and Big Ben strikes the hours that fly
at Westminster where all do vie
though all are not
discerning.
Neo-gothic walls and towers
overlook a court – no flowers –
and see, for her a dark cloud lours,
the Lady who is not
for turning.

The fight for leadership is won,
the Thatcher years have now begun,
a sure-fire winner myth is spun
when the Iron Lady she's become,
good repute is what
she's earning.
But through a mirror dark she sees,
believes in truths which her do please –
all else, she thinks, is newsroom sleaze,
the Lady who is not
for turning.

Who has not seen her wave her hand
to well-versed devotees who stand,
her every gesture clearly planned?
She's surely known throughout the land
and fresh acclaim is what
she's yearning.
With high-wave hair, crisply lacquered,
tailored voice with pet words smattered,
even bombs leave her unshattered,
the Lady who is not
for turning.

When in full stride who can restrain her
now Willie Whitelaw, old retainer,
is no longer there to tame her?
Others though would like to brain her
when their views are what
she's overturning.
Her sturdy handbag clasp snaps shut
a sign to ministers who strut.
I am full sick of slackers, tuts
the Lady who is not
for turning.

She's at her desk both night and day,
her true-blue vision under way.
A wicked rumour she's heard say:
a curse will mark her should she stay.
Inside she feels a knot,
a churning.
She knows not what the plot will be
but she won't budge, not one degree
and so she worketh slavishly,
the Lady who is not
for turning.

Yet up and down the lobbies go
her henchmen – be they friend or foe.
She sneers and calls some wet – but lo!
her man will strike the fatal blow –
of this she's sadly not
discerning.
Her nostrils flare, her lips slit wide,
her blue eyes flame. *No, no!* she'll chide
and sweeps those *losers* quite aside,
the Lady who is not
for turning.

Sir Geoffrey, mild and round of face
with owlish specs, shows her no trace
of disrespect or lack of grace
and yet he finds, being slow of pace,
this tyrant swot
concerning.
Though loyal knight, old-fashioned blue,
a calm man in the worst to-do,
she pecks him like a cockatoo,
the Lady who is not
for turning.

*Make way, Geoffrey, stand behind me.
It's me, you know, they want to see.*
Her finger wags impatiently.
At last he broke, vowed to be free.
He'd had his lot!
Such spurning!
Damn! and *Bother!* By the river
swore Sir Geoffrey, didn't dither,
boldly cursed her in the mirror,
the Lady who was not
for turning.

His speech resigning made all quiver,
little gasps drew little shivers
as he cut her into slivers.
Deep he sliced, right to her liver.
She'd soon be gone and not
returning.
All listened to the good knight's tale,
the Iron Lady she turned pale
but still her poise it did not fail,
the Lady who was not
for turning.

She left her bag, she left her room,
she took neat paces to her doom.
Sir Geoffrey's words had made her fume
as new PMs began to loom –
and she could spot
their turning.
Now for blood the pack bayed nightly,
thronging tightly, teeth bared slightly,
they brought her down, the kill unsightly,
the Lady who was not
for turning.

Her iron mask cracked from side to side,
tears trembled that she could not hide
and all she valued choked and died.
How could it end like this? she sighed,
*now they don't give a jot
I'm not returning.*
She wept farewell to Number Ten
but gave cold shoulder to her men.
The curse had come upon her then,
the Lady who was not
for turning.

To Dulwich she was borne away
(the *dragon* they would never slay!),
the skies of London turned quite grey
for suddenly she'd had her day –
squibs from the plot
still burning.
Sir Geoffrey, musing by the mace,
was saddened by her softer face
of which before she'd shown no trace,
the Lady who was not
for turning

Verdict

Women here hide behind scarves, walls and fear.
Though some start to lie, she's free of such guile.
Her son he seems kind but his male voice is clear.

With arms pinned behind, not shedding a tear,
Swathed all in black, she tries a half-smile.
Women here hide behind scarves, walls and fear.

Her lover is dead but their love was sincere.
She now awaits judgement, vote-without-trial –
her son feels torn but his rough voice is clear.

The trees are in blossom but fruit won't appear
until she departs, which will be in a while.
Women here lurk behind scarves, walls and fear.

He longs to forgive her but the mob starts to jeer.
Stones fly, blood blooms on a small crumpled pile.
Her son he seems kind but his male voice is clear.

He cradles the body, hoping all will revere
the grave which he hunts for, mile after mile.
Women here lurk behind scarves, walls and fear.
Though some sons feel torn, the male voice rings clear.

on Airforce One

Where's the smoking gun?
Whether you find it or no,
ride him outta town!

You folks know he's bad –
we've gotta trash him, smash him
ride him outta town!

the president

peddles tabloid truths,
tells folks watch the foe without but
don't watch reflections.

night poem

Most poems stay on the page,
This one won't lie down,
jumps up and shakes me awake,
kicks me into words.

election

booths empty, stubs break,
twilight voting ends;
feet tap to march.

stepping

Put a window in a poem, he says.
Why not a door to step through?

Put a window and a door perhaps –
would it still be a poem?

Put a window and a door – put a soul.
Look in; step into; pass through.

Find an image for the soul – let it soar.
                  Stop. No more.

VIII

Mrs Dribbles and the Chrome Invasion

Newly clamped and screwed into a stiff and shaky life,
Mrs Dribbles waits to see the silver-white gleam
of the aids-for-the-disabled that nightly stab,
graze or scratch her like knives in the night.
Crabby at her own feebleness, her head is pounding.

With family instructions not to shuffle, not to stoop,
not to give up, fumbling towards her forbidden bath,
she grabs the long-handled pincers to retrieve a towel.
How she longs, not for the chill brightness of chrome,
but for the unfolding warmth of a large g & t in the tub.

Mrs D knows she'd been colonised but can't
believe that the *not-yet time* has actually come.
Outside, the moon lights the here-and-now of a world
under snow. Only a fork-handle pokes through,
bent backwards to make her laugh.

Mrs Muddles and the Muddly Day

Can it be Tuesday today? Mrs M squints at her all-singing, all-dancing, eight-stop pill alarm (from which no current peep) and wonders what happened to the rest of exercise Monday?

They'd said she had to come off her previous pills because they might cause confusion in the elderly. Her consultant has prescribed a syrup but now she discovers in the blurb:

Over 65s should take less for fear of...confusion. Has she heard this before? Time to consult The Man. He smiles down the phone: *If I held back on every drug that causes confusion, Mrs M,*

I shouldn't be prescribing at all. Mrs Muddles is more confused. Would that be so bad? she ponders. Am I still sane but muddled or is something lurking on the line, something unnamed?

Consultants may smile. They're never confused. Or not much.

Mrs Wobbly is Fed Up

Mrs Wobbly, friend to Mrs Dribbles, is sick of falls, breakages,
not sleeping. Sick of balance routines, dribbling, a leaky bladder

and consultants with damn silly names no-one can remember.
She's fed up with trying not to hurry; not to multi-task;

fed up when her feet freeze or stumble or fall over each other
with nothing she can do about the downward spin, even if it's not

the head-first, go-directly-to-hospital type. On the hard floor-tiles
she feels broken in a million pieces – like her pride.

If I Had Pills Enough...

Had I the dopamine to waste,
and no regard for Time's great haste,
I'd wink and dance and have a fling –
you'd find me up for anything –
but at my back these days I hear
new blister packs pop at my ear.
With dribbling chin, stiff limbs, lost tone,
am I still me? For long? Not known.

Pain at Midnight

The pen tears poetry out of pain,
pain out of poetry with plasters
that strip skin bare. Fistfuls
of nettle-burns and word-weeds
sting, a deep-rooted wildness.

Surgeons' blades slice, stitch, fold
like bedding neatened by day
that by night pulls and tips
into a messy, tangled knot.
The song of hurt halts everything –

even the flow of sugared tea –
dressings, blood-maps
of distress, are ripped away.
The pain tears into the poetry
and the poetry into the pain

What If

I wake one morning, pillow
patchworked with wet, a salty
chocolate beard glazing my chin;

or ambushed by shakes, I spill
the pills I'm breaking, then
find I can't swallow them;

or my writing is squeezed and shrunk,
small as an elf's, reduced
to near invisibility?

What if my voice has slipped further
under the duvet, grown muffled
in the night so no-one can hear;

or, leg-locked, I can no longer swing
my long, cramping limbs out of
this Queen-sized island-prison?

What if, caged, I can't rest, read, sleep,
speak – can't remember who you are –
or who I am? What if

I don't now exist
as

Suppose

I can't convey

to outsiders that I'm locked behind bars,
my sense of self confiscated on entry,
a mere imposter able only to gurgle like

a drain blocked in a solitary cell?
or how wakeful winds of spontaneity
and a moon-bright light of intelligence

are blown away, fading as if they never were?
Suppose weir waters close over smiles
to un-face me so there are no landmarks

left to direct anyone to my loss,
and all is blankness, protests
under-voiced, less than a whisper to

trouble routine? When speech that bubbled
like a stream is no longer heard, what
is it that silence will say?

Don't

Don't dribble on your cashmere, dear,
don't stain the wool.
Don't shiver – that's a sign of fear.
Don't be a fool.
Don't mumble in your beer, dear.
Plain speech is the rule.
Does she take sugar? Be sincere –
stay clear, stay cool.

If your life is your own to steer, dear,
and your kids are your own to rear;
if you're happy with how you appear
and you don't give a toss or a tear,
get in gear, luv, give a cheer, luv.

Here, dear – don't dribble on your cashmere!

It

Unseen, it grows and spreads.
You grow a wig and a bigger smile.
Healing, homeopathy – even chemotherapy –

you engage with them all.
Though the wig starts to fit, you sense
the thing's return. It enters your house,

peeks into private corners of all kinds,
looks down drains, pokes out grates, wriggles
into every sag in the mattress.

It multiplies, filling lungs and liver. You drive
it out of one gap; smartly it slides in
through another. You pronounce yourself free,

the one that got away, a statistic never reached.
We still expect you to age gracefully,
turning to us with that dirty laugh of yours.

You're unaware of the shadow behind you.
Now your wispy smile is tight-lipped.
Nothing fits; everything sparks with pain.

We weep over your thrashing body until you leave it;
then for a week hold vigil round you,
in the end gently brushing away the summer maggots

bender
(a 14-word sonnet)

burp
pick-up
slurp
hiccup.
more
drinking
poor
thinking

smashed
lout
crashed
out,
blown
alone

work

When pay-cheque years end,
they find in midlife
new ways of seeing.

hospital bed

High platform on wheels,
Tube hang undone. Blood signs gone.
Crisp white sting of death.

geriatric

No-one notices:
hand-pocketed, full of pins,
he can only fall.

night-drop

Each bath drowns a friend.
Books tail-spin from late-hour grip,
bombed by sudden sleep.

IX

face

Must put on my face,
she'd tell us in the morning;
never at night-time.

angled

Saying nothing. Slowly.
Shoulders stiff-angled. Lips starched,
caught in a crisp pleat of disapproval.
Love folded away like best linen,
not to be soiled by everyday insults.

mother

M oments when no-one else will do
O therwise I shrink to age six – a year waiting,
T wisted in tears under scullery slabs
H ow will it be when you die?
E very Christmas there you are in your chair
R eading *The Telegraph*, mending my skirts.

no mother

N ibbling nails, six years old, wondering where you are
O r thinking of ringing you on birthdays or news-days

M eaning to tell you what I wouldn't when you were really there
O ver a cup of tea, no milk for you, bread and jam for me.
T hough your shape-space lingers, the warmth of you doesn't;
H ow empty the world feels now you've stone-cold gone.
E very evening, sixish, my mind reverts to the wire between us,
R emembering how you'd see the best in me – and the worst.

The Hat

My mother wore a black hat to my wedding, pinned
down with a sharp silver thistle. It wasn't the fancy
tam-o'-shanter or deep-pink pill-box I expected,
nor the floppy-brimmed, Derby Day sensation, or even

the single cream flower in lemon lace. No. *I'm a snob
and proud of it!,* she snapped, frowning, tone tailored
to her dark mood, while the funeral hat sat, snug with
velvet trim, riding the well-groomed waves of her hair.

Its low sweep couldn't hide the pale pinch of her face,
clenched around crisp-thin lips; and didn't disguise
the blow-darts of displeasure she launched
at the new in-laws, *those barbarians from the North.*

Refusing to froth down the aisle in white, on the arm
of a shining knight of her choice, maybe caused
her black mood. These days she smiles at my ruby ring
while her grandchildren play with the hat.

Mum Comes with Me to Therapy

When I asked I was sure you'd say *no*
with a cool and uncomfortable shrug.
In fact you were so sure you'd go,
it felt like you gave me a hug.

Up early you came on the dot –
curiosity making you keen.
En route we found a good picnic spot
(a *good-enough* lay-by, I mean).

You climbed up the outside staircase,
which I'd slipped on myself before now.
Though ninety, you went at a purposeful pace –
I inwardly made you a bow.

At first we none of us knew what to do,
this being for all three a first,
so you and I made a start with the loo –
without which, things would've got worse.

Our therapist, I must say, was grand
(not for nothing *doyenne* of her day);
Smiling, she took us in hand,
asked what was it vital to say?

Like pros, we set off at a lick,
shared thoughts on the past straight away,
soon judging my father yet more of a prick
than either had thought till this day.

An hour on, we'd learned quite a lot:
all three, I sensed, brimming with awe –
we'd hung in, not lost the plot –
and left the door open for more.

As you came down those fairy-tale stairs,
I felt proud, Mum, warm and impressed.
After brief therapeutic repairs,
you've gone home again now for your rest.

The Good Ship Care

What she hates is their being in charge, invading
her ship-shape home, her kingdom. Unforgiveable
the lack of Navy discipline. Her mouth-set decides
strength and direction of prevailing wind.

She is the captain of this ship but the captain's table,
hub of all social influence, is already disbanded.
The digital revolution has re-charted the seas.
She knows precisely what she wants – yet often orders
are flouted so she drifts away, insisting on insistence.

Life is reorganised by able- or less able-bodied seamen
or -women and deck littered with hoists, mugs,
a bed that tips. Unbiddable, these sailors won't cook,
demand time off to suit themselves, resist lifting her,
spend all their free time online, noses in computers.
And they have the nerve to impose their timetable on hers.

She complains to the duty officer. Nothing changes.
In the ship's log the captain records that they're sinking
but refuses to struggle into a care-home lifeboat or wriggle
into same brand of life-jacket. Having failed to out-boss
the bosses, she stays by her porthole, g & t in hand,
head held high, hair coiffed, gold chain in place.

As the sun bleeds into the evening sky she glides further
and further below the water line until finally learning
to cast them off and mastermind the going down of the sun
– and of the ship – her own personal flag-ship.

A Time to Die?

Time to meet my Maker, you whisper, and this time
I believe you. Fair enough, I think
as you open your eyes to check we're all there.

Give me a potion – I want to die, you insist.
Am I the only wicked witch who wants to organise
the spell you need? I fly down the ward

to an unmanned nursing station that glints
with greetings and tinsel and, as I search for help, wonder
why the hospital's so empty if no-one's allowed to die.

My family's busy unpacking Christmas – as you like it –
chocolates and crackers, gin and twiglets,
foil-wrapped presents, hottie and clean nightie.

Want a mince pie, Gran? the much-loved grandson urges
with a gurgle of delight, his sister's face soft and wet,
running with merriment as well as misery.

You don't want to die in here! prompts my partner,
his voice Machiavellian. You shift in your adjustable bed.
Tinsel truths seem to be the order of the day.

I observe now the hospital does have trolleys and porters for
the final exodus, but not on demand – and not on Boxing Day.
Calendars and balloons, baubles and streamers, yes;

death, no. As though this season were the wrong one,
apologies pour from you now as abundantly as your exit-pleas
flowed before. Is another spell at work?

The hospital looks on with a purr of satisfaction.
Keep up the antibiotics is the answer in here.
Living is all, they believe, even at ninety-two.

Grab-Handle

In the shower you cling to me, your new grab-handle.
Ignoring my shakes, we both pretend you're in safe hands.
Ninety years of fair usage, Mum, and your scrap of a body

is shrunken against a cage of chrome bars. Buttocks swing,
their skin an overhang of ragged sack; dugs hang
like empty toothpaste tubes; hip bones jut like garden stakes.

As if flicking a switch, before I can distance or disown them,
wartime images flash on my inner eye, a film-reel
of Pathé horrors. I feel the panic in your grip pinch

when I regulate the shower temperature, causing overflow.
I sense a warder's buzz of control
knowing you are lost in a huddle of hurt and helplessness.

Though eager for the rush of water to relax your greying skin,
you're fearful of falls, bruises, broken bones. Should you now
be fearful of me too? Frailty lays a hand on both of us,

each clutching at her hopes. Under the metallic power jets,
I scrub myself to clean my shame away and find the love that,
tight as a rosebud un-blossoming in winter, refused to flower today.

Just Before Dark

I tip-toe past our twilight hug, sneak round
the raw-boned set of your jaw and avoid you,
enthroned in your orthopaedic armchair,
translucent and fragile as crested bone china,
not broken but much cracked. I try to loop
my arm about you, Mum, only to see it drop
into the hollow space that once offered me
a feather-filled neck-and-shoulder pillow.

Scared to be left, as a child I'd lasso you home,
clinging to your cardigan to keep you in my hoop.
My head would burrow and butt your stomach;
bitten nails pat familiar powdered cheeks;
nose snuffle the comfort of chestnut curls.

We stuck together then like stacked saucers;
now the jut of blade-sharp shoulder-bones blocks
that snug fit. Yet somewhere deep love lingers.
As night falls my fingers stroke indigo-stained flesh
under the regal flounce of soft mauve wool, and reach
into your sleeve to greet you, a carcass in cashmere.

Uncharted

Your bone-hard mouth, like an open cave,
seaweed stretched over jagged rock-teeth,
gulps at the tide that sucks, in and out,
breathing rough, insistent spray. I hold
your drowning hand so tight blood drains
from it in white waves as if I were the parent,
you the child stranded in nightmare seas.

In the wreckage of lost life I don't know who
or where you are, or if you know me at all.
I too am wrecked, a stranger to this vast ocean.
Muscles tighten and cramp, fearful
at your going, so far beyond my horizon.
Still, I hope my grip steadies you, that you feel
its squeeze, take in my muttered lovings.

Here by your bedside I want to call you home
though already you're panting to push through
the storm's growl and I'm rowing the wreckage,
hand clutched to fleshless claw, trying
to stay up and keep the rhythm of the stroke until
fingers twine around the rightness of your going,
reconciled at last to the distance between us.

Dying is a challenging business.
Over the crashing foam I cry out to you:
I'm here. Don't worry, Mum. I'll stay right here.
Hours later, though, I break my word and have
to leave your side. You let your grasp loosen
and, out of reach now, sink down alone
to the rock below, the uncharted sea-bed.

X

Throssel Hole

Buddhist Monastery

Flowers fill the bed
round the pond where water flows
yet space is still found.

*

Pale sun trickles in
as though it were winter now
not rabbit-patch summer.

*

The midges grow worse,
skin an irritable red
peace swatted away.

*

Japanese elders
in slippage of pink and white,
froth flowing downhill.

*

A statue ponders,
guarded by tall irises
holding silent space.

*

Flowers make colour
round the pond where water flows
seeking quiet space.

Walking Backwards

Cloud fans down the valley,
darkening the patchwork of pink soil, copper fern
and emerald larch stitched

with a scattering of lambs,
behind which the Black Mountains bare their backs
to the spring sky.

The wind tackles and tugs.
Think backwards, move forwards, the physio would say,
so why, here in the Welsh Marches,

am I bending into gusts that swirl
and swerve like skids to be steered into?
To trick the brain, I could soften,

lengthen to full height.
My back smiles, a place of witness from which dopamine
– what's left of it – kicks in.

Unlike lambs who tumble,
loose around this rough pasture, I stumble on, nudging
a paradox in which

forward is back and back forward.
It's not the journey of a few fumbling steps I face.
It's the journey of a thousand backward limps.

Note: The Alexander Technique is a way of encouraging flowing movement particularly useful to people with neurological conditions such as Parkinson's when running out of dopamine may lead to freezing. The sufferer can use learned neurological tricks to facilitate more movement.

God Is

not unkind enough to make prayer a condition of sleep
not fashionable enough to sport own-design labelling
not obvious enough to be seen through a glass darkly

nor trite enough to be glimpsed in a flash of sunset
not sensible enough to attract belief without doubt
nor regular enough to deliver daily bread or cake

not quick enough to forgive all our mistakes
not economical enough with bad news
not small enough to write about

not trusted enough to cry for
not there not when
not then

God is

Eagle Wings

carve a wide fan,
the vast lectern
waking to judgement,
leather bible, gripped
talon-tight like prey.

Quick eyes burn
with precision brightness,
poised to swoop, a search beam
for all small tremblers
called to account today.

Seven Deadly Sins

pride
    Climb past garbage. Breathe
        fine air on spacious summit
            zipped against contact.

gluttony
    Undress crabs, squeeze rolls,
        gorge breast meat, suck juice from tarts.
        Throw up as usual

anger
    Poker-bright, hot-pointed,
        grab him, stab. Sizzle of skin.
            Smell your own hand burn.

greed
    Grub out silver, plant
        your gold. Rake ripe coins. Stack high.
            Fence and pant for more.

envy
    A buzz in the brain,
        static of wanting. *Why not*
            me? hums in the head.

lust
    Cream of flesh cooking,
        beach-scented, dripping. Hot sin.
            Lick and scoff the lot.

sloth
    Won't move now. Later.
        Later's too soon – so – never.
            Tip into sleep. Sleep

Riddle

I'm the clutch of a baby's finger
un-petalling in your hand;
the scent of scentless roses when
all is thorn and gone to seed;

I'm the clover-leaf never found,
the horseshoe not picked up;
the game of hopscotch
where fate hovers in every leap;

or the near-miss of meteorites
hurtling towards our planet;
or a boy overboard, out of reach
while white sands wait for a body;

I'm a one-way road, surfaced
with the debris of collective crashing;
the iron staircase that spirals
rung-less into space;

I'm a small word, a cliché almost,
constant reinvention of myself –
I drift colourfully into metaphor,
return to straight translation;

I am not death, nor is it me;
yet, we are joined at the hip
and come and go together –
noisy as newborns and silent as stillbirth.

El Alcazar

Early fingers of sun
pattern the Moorish courtyard
tiled in peacock blue.

Through the high-hipped arch
sun beckons, reminding us
of old hopes dreaming.

Fountain and silence
commune under the arches,
fill the midday space –

such a small fountain,
its frail stream a mere burble of peace
to a passing world.

Above, pigeons sulk
where fine Spanish portraits hang.
Tourists tramp cold floors.

How wise the masters
not to configure form,
human or divine,

but wait rather on motifs
or on patterning that glows like
the face of eternity

Just Sitting

at a Buddhist Monastery in Northumberland

Stunned by the mockery in your motorway voice,
your rage breaking over me, swallowing
my tiny figure in flight, I head north to search for

that space where pace slows and silence speaks.
The Abbey's drive twists through ill-tempered rain,
passes a fat stone Buddha smiling through tall grass.

I'm haunted by your fury at the shuffling, grumbling,
mumbling, stumbling – forgetting – mess that is me.
Your playing *Dare* in the fast lane keeps returning

like the memory of an electric shock shocking.
Outside the great hall, rabbits, tamed by kindness,
grow fat on fresh weeds; inside, monks fill the place

with order as they process, fold and align mats,
light candles, offer up their care and sit in *zazen**
so the huge hall is rich with the sound of quietness.

In the long light of evening meditation I want
a still mind, not the din of judgements tussling within.
Just sit, says the monk, looking at the rabbits.

**Note: zazen – the Zen term for sitting in meditation*

Walking Meditation

Circling the hall with barefoot diligence,
I pace out my distracted thoughts,

brimming with yesterday's chat,
overflowing with worries,

sorrys or tomorrow's menu for
the long soap opera of the mind.

As I tread the carpet pile,
a flash of knowing brightens the room:

NOW

is the sudden sun washing my face –
I am its never-ending warmth:

NOW

is the give of wool, soft beneath my feet –
I become that forever stretch of silence

until

The Present Moment

For a brief second, I'm inside
the perfection of the moment,
realising and seeing myself
delighted at the achievement.

Now there is only imperfection
of the lost moment, but not all is lost –
I'm learning about me, my longings,
my desire to peep under the lens,

to peer at the dish of surgical parts
going under analysis as though
observing and understanding
could somehow find

the now, which is not lost
and is always perfect in the forgetting.

Arches

Your long drive is done
car keys back on the hook
still tagged with your name and number.
You will not take them down again.

The calendar you purchased in Seville
hangs there too. On its cover
the Alhambra Palace, a gem
glowing, Moorish, its mountains crossed.

You've lost the dimension of days,
weeks, months which it logs
and tries to contain; already passed
through the evening fire of arches.

You have outgrown me, gone on
like the flight of swifts to explore
beyond the geometry of destination
to a space that can't be known

where snow-steps loop and trail away,
leaving only the sound of fountain-spray
that lifts and arches over,
drifting into distant silence.

Other titles available to order

(A contribution to Parkinson's research will be made for each copy sold.)

The Now of Snow by June Hall (Belgrave Press)

'Read *The Now of Snow* NOW for both pleasure and enlightenment.' **U A Fanthorpe**

Published 2004   64pp.   Laminated paperback   £7.99

Bowing to Winter by June Hall (Belgrave Press)

'Truth is the cornerstone of her writing.' **Ann Drysdale**

Published 2010   80pp.   Laminated paperback   £7.99

Uncharted by June Hall (Belgrave Press)

'June Hall writes vividly and well about almost everything that frightens us.' **Dilys Wood**

Published 2016   112pp   Laminated paperback   £9.99

The Book of Love & Loss
(Belgrave Press, ed. by R V Bailey and June Hall)

'A pace-maker for the broken heart.' **Maureen Lipman**

Published 2014   384pp   Hardback   £12.99

Check with bookshops/the internet for current ordering info, or with email:halljunep@gmail.com